Louis I. Kahn

Joseph Rosa

LOUIS I. KAHN

1901–1974

Enlightened space

KÖLN LONDON LOS ANGELES MADRID PARIS TOKYO

Picture page 2 ▶ Louis I. Kahn at his drafting table, 1961
Picture page 4 ▶ Indian Institute of Management, Ahmedabad, India, Sketch, 1964

© 2006 TASCHEN GmbH
Hohenzollernring 53, D-50672 Köln
www.taschen.com

Editor ▶ Peter Gössel, Bremen
Project management ▶ Swantje Schmidt, Bremen
Design and layout ▶ Gössel und Partner, Bremen
Text edited by ▶ Christiane Blass, Cologne

Printed in Germany
ISBN 3-8228-3641-9

Contents

Introduction

There have been very few moments in the history of architecture when a single building has signaled a shift in the future direction of the discipline. Louis I. Kahn's 1951–1953 Yale University Art Gallery addition achieved that status by marking the arrival of monumentality in American modern architecture.

Historically, critical architectural thinking can be divided into two simple categories: one that promotes, refines, and implements previous rhetoric; and the other that represents a rupture in the current ideology that reveals a new direction. While the first furthers a certain ideology, producing mostly mainstream examples, the latter usually results in more inventive work that sets a new course in the pedagogy and practice of architecture. The legacy of Kahn's ideology places him in the inventive category, making him one of the most important American architects of the twentieth century since Frank Lloyd Wright. Kahn was never truly part of the mainstream aesthetic of the International Style, but, rather, embraced historical precedents to inform his design process, which resulted in a new ideological architectural model.

Kahn's brilliance lay in the fact that he operated on the fringe of the International Style and was not fully involved in it. It was only later in his professional life, at the age of fifty that his career took off after spending time abroad at the American Academy in Rome in 1950–1951—when a new course was set for his career as well as for the future of modern architecture.

To better understand how Kahn's Yale University Art Gallery addition became such a pivotal building in his career, as well as in architectural history, one needs to look at the context in which architecture had evolved by mid-century in America. Two decades earlier, during the celebrated 1932 exhibition "Modern Architecture: International Exhibition"—curated by Philip Johnson and Henry-Russell Hitchcock at the Museum of Modern Art in New York—its catalogue (of the same title) as well as their book *The International Style: Architecture since 1922*, officially marked the arrival of this European aesthetic to American shores. After being held in New York, the show traveled for the next two years to more than fourteen additional venues throughout the United States, showcasing prime examples of this new avant-garde aesthetic.

While the exhibition contained mostly European examples and only a few American ones, it was for many the first exposure to the works of such architects as Ludwig Mies van der Rohe, Le Corbusier, and Walter Gropius, who became known as modern masters of this new "machined" aesthetic. By the mid-to-late 1930s—with the rise of Hitler and Nazism spreading throughout Europe—many progressively minded European architects emigrated to the United States, where they took up academic posts. The institutionalization of the International Style as a codifiable new aesthetic for the pedagogy and practice of architecture in America occurred owing to Mies van der Rohe having taught at the School of Architecture at the Illinois Institute of Technology (then the Armour Institute), Chicago in 1938, and Gropius having taught at Harvard's Graduate School of Design in Cambridge, Massachusetts in 1937 (assuming the department chair in 1938). Academic programs began to reject traditional Beaux-Arts

Louis I. Kahn: Townscape, Positano, Italy, 1929
Watercolor on paper

teaching methods, which embraced styles of the past. This progressive ideology led to significant aesthetic achievements in architecture; however, because these historical styles were no longer part of university curricula, modern students of architecture were left with a gap in their education. What was lost was an understanding of classical proportions and a sense of European history from antiquity to the nineteenth century.

As the International Style matured, the notion of monumentality in modern architecture came into play. In 1938, in his book *The Culture of Cities*, architectural historian and critic Lewis Mumford raised the point succinctly: "if it is a monument it is not modern, and if it is modern it cannot be a monument." The modern aesthetic had evolved into a viable style and was antithetical to the notion of monumentality; yet the way architecture beyond the domestic scale was designed, such as large-scale civic and public buildings, would still need to be addressed.

Needless to say, by the early 1940s, monumentality became a growing issue in the discipline. One of the most influential essays on this topic was "Nine Points on Monumentality," authored by architectural historian Sigfried Giedion, architect Josep Luís Sert, and artist Fernand Léger, and published with a collection of essays on the subject in *New Architecture and City Planning* of 1944, edited by Paul Zucker. Another lesser-known contributor to the publication was Kahn, with his essay "Monumentality." Whereas Giedion, Sert, and Léger call for a reevaluation of modern architecture's recent past to construct a framework within which a new monumentality could operate without historical precedents, Kahn addresses the more interpretive, introspective, and spiritual aspects of monumentality, embracing the past in order to discover future possibilities:

"No architect can rebuild a cathedral of another epoch, embodying the desires, the aspirations, the love and hate of the people whose heritage it became. Therefore the images we have before us of monumental structures of the past cannot live again with the same intensity and meaning. Their faithful duplication is unreconcilable. But we dare not discard the lessons these buildings teach, for they have the common characteristics of greatness upon which the buildings of our future must, in one sense or another, rely."

In this theoretical statement we can discern the origins of Kahn's ideology as well as his later methodology and architectural productions that embrace historical precedents.

As the "progressive" aesthetic of the International Style became the normative style taught and practiced in the United States and Europe, it also started to show signs that it had run its course from its radical avant-garde origins to its mainstream application as a corporate style. Not surprisingly, many architectural periodicals—and even New York's Museum of Modern Art in its 1948 symposium "What Happened to Modern Architecture?"—raised the question: What is the next modern? This was a valid question concerning an aesthetic movement that was conceived as a rigid system of "form follows function" and that appeared incapable of evolving.

However, by mid-century, a new generation of architects—students of these European masters at American universities—became noted figures in the discipline, such as Gordon Bunshaft, Edward Durell Stone, and Philip Johnson. Many projects by these architects illustrate a shift in the aesthetic production of large civic and public buildings. This resulted in a contextual "decorative" aesthetic consisting of brise-soleils or abstract patterned surfaces to modulate the rather austere lines of the buildings and

Louis I. Kahn: Temple Ruins, Egypt, 1951
Pastel

their lobbies. Yet, many critics who believed in the doctrine of "form follows function" viewed this later shift as a decline in the ideology, citing buildings by Bunshaft, Stone, and Johnson as "vulgar" architecture. Although this "decorative" aesthetic was derided in architectural periodicals and books, it became the prevalent style of civic, institutional, and public buildings for two decades. In retrospect, the criticism leveled against this generation and its attempt at monumental architecture is best summed up by William J. R. Curtis in his 1982 book *Modern Architecture Since 1900*:

"In the United States the expansive, optimistic, and indeed, imperial undercurrents of the post-war years were manifest in many commissions for large-scale monuments. The influence of the Beaux-Arts classicism certainly did not die with the introduction of modern architecture [...]. This was no doubt part of a general mood of dissatisfaction with the restrictive minimalism of the American version of the International Style. Thus architects like Stone, Johnson, Harrison and Abramovitz, indulged in grand axes, symmetry, expensive materials or telltale arches, to disguise an essentially bogus and skindeep understanding of the nature of monumentality. These architects were well aware of the need to combine traditional schemata with modern technology, but were still unable to transcend a tendency towards 'camp.' Classical allusions were there in abundance; classical principles were almost entirely lacking."

Architects who were the products of American "modern" architectural pedagogy could not operate on a monumental scale simply because they lacked knowledge of classical principles, which, when they tried to implement them, resulted only in their being misconstrued. However, for Curtis, Kahn's work suggests "a new direction for American modern architecture" that can embrace the past in order to generate a new architectural ideology that can achieve monumentality when desired:

"The master of monumentality, without a doubt, [was] Kahn. Monumentality was not, of course, his only preoccupation, but it was certainly a major one, and he evolved a philosophy and system of forms extraordinarily well suited to the expression of honorific themes and moods [...]. Kahn was capable of handling problems of large scale without degenerating into either an 'additive' approach or an overdone grandiosity [...] which enabled him to avoid the mere shape-making of the formalists."

Architecture comes from The Making of a Room The Plan A society of rooms is a place good to live work learn

A great American Poet once asked The Architect 'What slice of the sun does your building have, what light enter your Room as if to say the sun never knew how great it is until it struck The side of a building.

The Room

is The place of the mind.. In a small room one does not say what one would in a large room. In a room with only one other person could be generalis The vectors of each meet. A room is not a room without natural light. natural light gives the time of day and the mood of The seasons To enter.

Kahn's addition to the Yale University Art Gallery signaled this shift in his thinking. From the triangular layout of the public stair within a cylindrical stairwell to the tetrahedron metal formwork for casting the concrete floor slabs, the design employed pure geometrical forms in its structural framework. The resulting spatial characteristics, while contemporary, contextualized the addition in the setting of the Victorian structure to which it was annexed. The building also reflects Kahn's time in Rome and further study of antiquity in Europe. Collectively, these events signaled a major shift in his ideology and practice, which made him a leading figure in American modern architecture who was able to reposition contemporary architectural pedagogy. Kahn's ability to operate within the realm of historical precedents filtered though a contemporary framework was in part due to his training as an architect. Kahn had not studied the modernist doctrine of the International Style, but had sound, traditional architectural training in the Beaux-Arts instead. It is precisely this aspect that allowed him to exist as a practitioner on the fringe of the International Style, emerging as a visionary leader by mid-century.

Kahn was born in 1901 in Estonia and moved with his mother, Bertha, and his siblings to the United States in 1906, settling in Philadelphia, where his father, Leopold, had immigrated to in 1904. Kahn received his diploma in architecture from the University of Pennsylvania in 1924, traveled to Europe in 1928, and returned to the United States to work for Paul P. Cret the following year. Cret was a leading Beaux-Arts

Right page:
Detailed exterior view of the Salk Institute for Biological Studies, La Jolla, California, 1959–1965

figure in America, whose buildings have beautiful proportions and a fine sense of scale. In 1941, Kahn formed a partnership with George Howe—one of the leading modern architects on the East Coast. Howe's earlier partnership with William Lescaze—which lasted from 1929 to 1934—produced some of the most important International Style buildings in America. Howe and Lescaze's 1929–1932 Philadelphia Savings Fund Society (PSFS) Building in Philadelphia was one of the first examples of a truly modern skyscraper and, hence, one of the few American entries in the 1932 "Modern Architecture: International Exhibition" at the Museum of Modern Art. Howe was Kahn's senior by fifteen years, and had Beaux-Arts training. Their collaboration led to less significant projects, however.

In 1941, Oscar Stonorov became a third partner in the firm, with Howe leaving the following year. It was Stonorov who introduced Kahn to the buildings and writings of Le Corbusier. During this brief collaboration between Howe, Stonorov and Kahn, the firm produced the Carver Court Housing Development in Coatesville, Pennsylvania, for the Federal Public Housing Authority. It illustrated a contextual modern vocabulary that would later be associated with Kahn's residential work.

Together, Stonorov and Kahn undertook a number of important housing projects; however, the aesthetic character of their work was never as well received as that of other modern architects practicing within the modern idiom. It was in 1947, the year he commenced teaching at the School of Architecture at Yale University, that Kahn began to be viewed as a wonderful educator, influencing a generation of architects to look at alternative frameworks, and slowly started to lecture and write on his ideology. In many ways, as a practitioner, Kahn operated under the radar until he was hired at Yale by

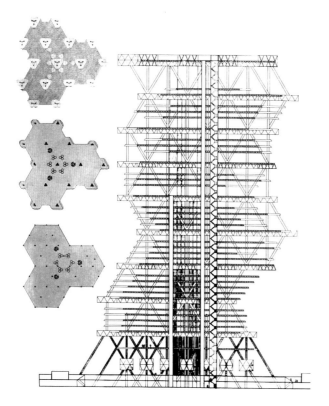

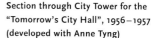

Section through City Tower for the "Tomorrow's City Hall", 1956–1957 (developed with Anne Tyng)

Howe—then Chair of the School of Architecture—to teach design studio. This, coupled with the commission for the Yale addition a few years later and his being awarded the prestigious Rome Prize, gave rise to a new Kahn who was fully equipped to pick up where the International Style had left off.

One of Kahn's staunchest supporters, who recognized the architect's ideological transformation, was architectural historian Vincent J. Scully. In Scully's 1962 book *Louis I. Kahn*, he poignantly describes Kahn's shift from the sidelines to center stage:

"Ten years ago Louis I. Kahn, then over fifty, had built almost nothing and was known to few people other than his associates in Philadelphia and his students at Yale. None of them would at that time have called him great, although his students generally felt, with some uneasiness, that he should have been, even might have been, so. But within ten years the 'might-have-been' has turned to 'is,' and Kahn's achievement of a single decade now places him unquestionably first in professional importance among living architects. His theory, like his practice, has been acclaimed as the most creative, no less than the most deeply felt, of any architect's today. He is the one architect whom almost all others admire, and his reputation is international."

Within the span of a decade, Kahn went from being virtually unknown to becoming an international architectural figure. His unbuilt and built works designed over the next two and a half decades bear witness to Kahn's brilliance as an architect. Until his death in 1974, he continued on this path, designing some of the most important buildings of the twentieth century.

Another building designed by Kahn (with his associate Anne Tyng) around the same time as the Yale University Art Gallery addition was the City Tower for the "Tomorrow's

City Hall" study (1952–1957). The unbuilt proposal lends insight into Kahn the visionary, who was more than willing to abandon the International Style to conceive a completely new notion of a contextual/critical modern architecture.

This triangulated skyscraper illustrates numerous aspects of Kahn's later aesthetic—most notably the serial form employed in the overall structural framework that
resulted in its megastructural characteristics. The City Tower also documents the
influence of Buckminster Fuller on Kahn's ideology vis-à-vis Tyng. On another level,
one can also see how this design became an "ideological" bridge between the avant-
garde thinking of Fuller of the 1930s in America to the later avant-garde movements
of the 1960s in Europe with *Archigram* and in Japan with *Metabolism*—where the idea
of multiplicity and monumentality resulted in megastructures that criticized and
mocked the modernist doctrine of "form follows function." This aspect of seriality—in
repetitive massing—and monumentality became an increasing characteristic of his
later work, which resulted in buildings comprised of ceremonial Euclidean forms. Be it
the pavilion-like forms that flank the courtyard of the Salk Institute in La Jolla, California, or the vast monolithic scale of the bilaterally symmetrical National Assembly
Building in Dhaka, Bangladesh, Kahn's buildings took architectural scale to new
spiritual heights.

Many of Kahn's large projects—specifically those for Pakistan and Bangladesh—
evoke a sense of timelessness. In fact, the massing of these designs became hypergeo-
metric and defied normative architectural scale, with vast circular or triangulated openings penetrating larger surfaces. On closer inspection, these shapes were made of
simple materials, such as brick or concrete, and had their own formal vocabulary. In an
interview with John W. Cook and Heinrich Klotz, in their book *Conversations with
Architects* of 1973—one year before Kahn's death—the architect addresses this aspect
of timelessness in materiality and purity in construction methods vis-à-vis brick and its
inherent characteristics:

Performing Arts Center, Fort Wayne, Indiana, 1961–1973
Rendering of the theater's main entrance façade

"It's the nature of masonry work. When you use brick you come to certain solutions which sometimes look like Roman brickwork, because brick is brickwork. I don't hesitate to do it, even if it does look Roman, because it's the order of brick. Where in Roman brickwork would you see a segmented arch, without having much buttressing of masonry? That restraining member made a composite order, brick and concrete. The use of concrete stems from knowing brick for what it is. I would never be able to do this, nor come to this realization, unless I respected brickwork in general, Roman or otherwise. Nobody possesses it. This is not a shape of any kind. It's not a motif. It's in the order of brick." Kahn's observations on materials are central to his essentialist ideology that enabled his work to be radically progressive yet surprisingly contextual and grounded in antiquity. In many ways, the clarity, complexity, and spirituality of Kahn's work were mirrored in his personal life and in the many young careers he influenced as an academic.

In the course of his life, Kahn had three children with three different women—the last of whom he remained married to until his death. In 1930, Kahn married Esther Virginia Israeli, who formed the foundation in his life. Their daughter, Sue Ann, was born in 1940. In the early 1950s, Kahn had a personal relationship with the most important design collaborator in his studio, Anne Griswold Tyng. (Tyng's influence on Kahn can be seen in many designs—starting with the 1951–1953 Yale University Art Gallery addition to the 1959 Jewish Community Center in Trenton, New Jersey.) Their daughter, Alexandra Tyng, was born in 1954. In Anne Tyng's 1997 book *Louis Kahn to Anne Tyng: The Rome Letters, 1953–1954*, which includes Kahn's letters to her when she went to Rome to give birth to their daughter, she reflects on their relationship: "Lou and I were lovers, but I was not his 'mistress.' I was uncomfortable with the idea of being 'owned'..."

Tyng started working for Kahn in 1945, when he was in partnership with Stonorov. By 1960, however, Tyng suggested that the relationship become "platonic," sensing

National Assembly Building of Sher-e-Bangla Nagar, Dhaka, Bangladesh, 1962–1983
Façade of mosque in foreground, with office buildings on left and right side. Parliament stands in background.

he was already involved with someone else. This new relationship was with another talented designer in his office, Harriet Pattison, who worked on another floor. Pattison played a major role in Kahn's 1972 Kimbell Art Museum in Fort Worth, Texas. Their son, Nathaniel Kahn, was born in 1963.

Both Tyng and Pattison stayed on as associates in Kahn's firm after their personal relationships had changed character. In many ways, Kahn's personal life revolved around three different households. This fractured personal life became ironic when he died suddenly in 1974. Kahn suffered a heart attack in the men's room at Pennsylvania Station in New York City. His only form of identification was his passport, in which, however, Kahn had crossed out his home address, rendering him a John Doe for three days until his office was able to trace his perambulations that day. The first time his children collectively saw each other was at his wake. However, it was not until two and a half decades later, when Kahn's youngest child, Nathaniel, produced a film entitled *My Architect* (2003) that they came together to talk about their childhood memories of their father.

Kahn's complex yet spiritually uncompromising way of life was what attracted people to the architect—his sense of intellect, strength, vision, and ideals came through in his person as well as his buildings and writings. The genius of Kahn is truly a rarity in the pedagogy and practice of architecture. His ideals, challenges, persistence, and vision, however, are best expressed by Kahn himself, at the conclusion of his 1944 essay "Monumentality," in which he speaks of those ideals that—thirty years later—he achieved:

National Assembly Building of Sher-e-Bangla Nagar, Dhaka, Bangladesh, 1962–1983
Sketch

"I do not wish to imply that monumentality can be attained scientifically or that the work of the architect reaches its greatest service to humanity by his peculiar genius to guide a concept toward a monumentality. I merely defend, because I admire, the architect who possesses the will to grow with the many angles of our development. For such a man finds himself far ahead of his fellow workers."

1939–1943 ▸ Oser House
Elkins Park, Pennsylvania

Plan

Commissioned by Jesse and Ruth Oser—good friends of Kahn and his wife, Esther—the house was built on a wooded hillside in Montgomery County; however, it was originally designed for another site in Melrose Park. This early dwelling by Kahn is a significant commission, which illustrates characteristics that later would become more evolved and indicative of his aesthetic. It is during the tenure of the Oser House that Kahn was invited to go into partnership with George Howe, in 1941, to work on public housing projects (later that year, they invited Oscar Stonorov to join the partnership).

Howe was one of the most important senior figures in American architecture on the East Coast, and he had a natural ability to find younger talented designers with whom to collaborate. The influence of Howe's aesthetic can be discerned somewhat in the Oser House, specifically in the type of windows used and their arrangement on the façades, as well as the employment of stone on the building's exterior. Howe had used these features in 1934 in his design for a vast estate called "Square Shadows" for Mr. and Mrs. William Stix Wasserman in Chestnut Hill, Pennsylvania.

Formally, the rectangular massing of the Oser House is clad in stone and any addition or subtraction to this overall massing is articulated in horizontal wood siding. This very simple gesture allows the changes in the building's massing surfaces to become visually associated with these different materials.

Right:
Living room with dining area beyond

Left page:
Exterior view of house in landscape

1941–1944 ▸ Carver Court Housing
Coatesville, Pennsylvania ▸ in collaboration with Howe and Stonorov

Left page:
Detailed view of exterior cladding

Overall street view of development

The first major introduction of Kahn's work to a larger public—prior to building the 1951–1953 Art Gallery addition at Yale University—was the Carver Court Housing Development. The realized project was featured in the 1944 exhibition "Built in USA: 1932–1944," curated by Elizabeth Mock and held at the Museum of Modern Art in New York. In the exhibition catalogue, Mock singles out this project as one of the few model solutions for modern "public" housing:

"If a number of houses are planned as a related group, how can unity be achieved without monotony? In larger groups of lower-cost houses, the effect depends upon a precarious balance of repetition and variety and upon careful design. Few housing projects have been as successful in this respect as [the Carver Court Housing Development in] Coatesville."

While the collaboration between Howe, Stonorov, and Kahn produced numerous public housing projects, Coatesville became their most visible and innovative for rethinking this building type and its planned community.

Located on a lightly wooded hillside, Carver Court comprised 100 housing units for war workers and their families. The development also had ancillary maintenance and administrative structures with public spaces that functioned during the day as a nursery for children, and in the evening as a public gathering place for parents. The site plan for the development is not laid out on a Cartesian grid, but rather on a gently curving single street that loops around the property and is flanked with housing units on either side. Four dwelling types were designed for the development, all of which were clad with horizontal wood siding. One of the most interesting dwelling types was the three-bedroom unit, in which all the living spaces were on the second floor, with an

View of second floor with kitchen beyond

entry, utility room, and carport at ground level. Supporting the wood-framed structure of these second floors were concrete block pier walls that added character and variety in height to these buildings in the landscape. The concrete block piers also lend a sense of scale and proportion, in addition to providing shade—an element that would recur in Kahn's later civic, public, and institutional commissions.

Exterior view of sun-shading device

Site plan

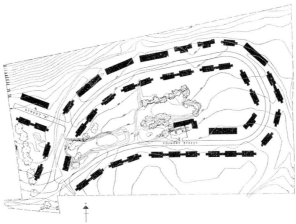

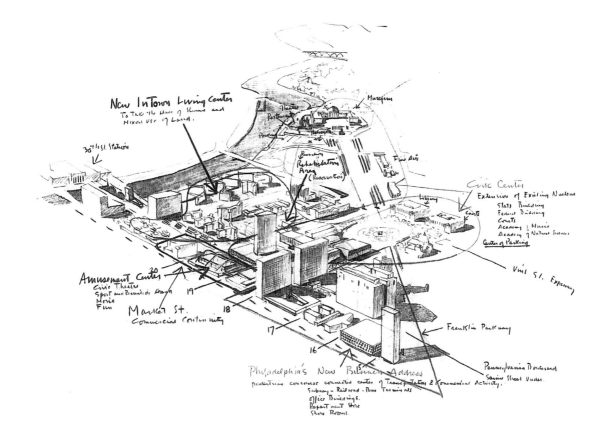

New In Town Living Center
To Take the place of Slums and
Mixed Use of Land.

30th St. Station

Amusement Center
Civic Theatre
Sport and Recreation Arena
Movie
Fun

Market St.
Commercial Continuity

Recreation
Rehabilitation
Area
(Reservation)

Museum

Theatre
Restaurant

Fine Arts

Civic Center
Extension of Existing Nucleus
State Building
Federal Building
Courts
Academy of Music
Academy of Natural Sciences
Center of Parking

Library

Courts

Vine St. Expressway

Franklin Parkway

Pennsylvania Boulevard
Spring Street Under

Philadelphia's New Business Address
pedestrian concourse connected center of Transportation & Commercial Activity.
Subway - Rail road - Bus Terminals
Office Buildings.
Department Store
Show Rooms.

Bird's-eye perspective of Triangle Area Redevelopment, ca. 1947

Philadelphia was Kahn's city, and throughout his career he made great efforts and innovative proposals to reconceive it. Aspects of his spatial thinking can be discerned in his numerous analytical drawings, some of which simply isolate vehicular traffic and reconfigure Philadelphia into a completely new, idealized city. Many of Kahn's abstract studies of circulation and city massing can be seen in his later realized National Assembly Building for the capital of Bangladesh as well as larger urban projects for ailing American cities.

One of Kahn's first projects was the "Triangle," a vast site in Philadelphia considered to be a blight location with vacant lots and dilapidated buildings. Kahn's proposal for the Triangle Area Redevelopment (1946–1948) was an ideal modern city with horizontal building blocks and a concourse traversing a large plaza.

By the early 1950s, Kahn became involved in rethinking traffic congestion and in the issue of how addressing this problem meant literally putting the city further into dis-

Left page:
Model Exhibit, Philadephia, 1947

Triangle Area Redevelopment, 1946–1948
Perspective of concourse, looking north toward
Suburb Station

Unbuilt Philadelphia City Planning, 1951–1953
Traffic Movement Study

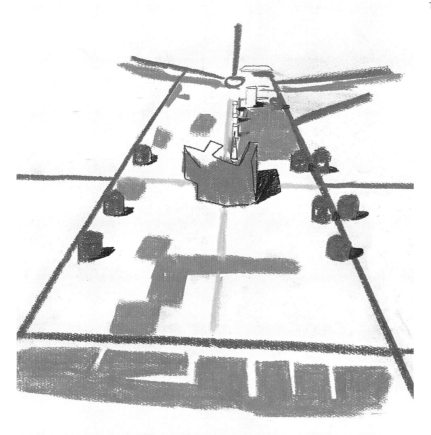

Civic Center, 1956–1957
Cutaway perspective of parking tower, ca. 1957

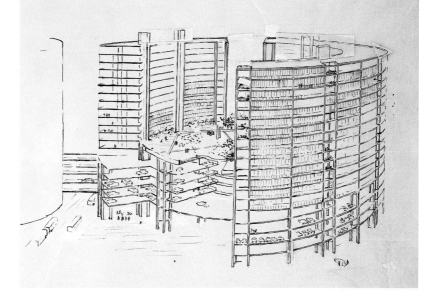

repair. One solution was to redirect traffic patterns by identifying streets for slower and faster-moving traffic. To illustrate these problematic conditions, as well as how his solution could resolve them, Kahn executed a series of drawings that include abstract notations of various modes of movement, be it vehicular or pedestrian. Kahn called his methodology the "Order of Movement", employing it as a device to regulate and analyze movement and to convey it visually.

Over the decades the city planning project for Philadelphia developed with new structures, public spaces, and areas for pedestrian as well as vehicular movement. Moreover, Kahn's ideas grew more visionary over time, and he entertained the notion of redirecting all vehicular traffic outside the city center. However, Edmund Bacon, the executive director of Philadelphia's City Planning Commission, did not view this as a realistic option. In late 1959, Kahn put forth another proposal that became known as "Viaduct Architecture," which surrounded the city center with multilevel viaducts that allowed for new, multiple patterns of movement throughout the city.

1951–1953 ▸ Yale University Art Gallery

New Haven, Connecticut

Perspective sketch from the southeast, showing the existing building and Kahn's addition

Kahn's Yale University Art Gallery is an addition to an existing 1928 gallery—designed by Edgerton Swartwout—on a campus largely consisting of neo-Gothic buildings. This elegant solution marked the arrival of Kahn as a designer who would not adhere to the then prevailing notion of "form follows function" so indicative of the International Style. The interior of the gallery is characterized by its vast open spaces with an expressive ceiling made of a triangular concrete pattern that conceals the lighting and mechanical systems above it. The triangle motif is reiterated in the concrete interior cylindrical stairwell. The exterior of the building comprises vast expanses of glass and is clad in brick with projected horizontal datums that delineate the interior floor plates. This relatively simple design reveals an architectural vocabulary that belongs to Kahn alone, more refined examples of which can be seen in some of the architect's later, larger buildings.

Kahn almost missed the opportunity to design Yale's first modern building. In 1941, Katherine S. Dreier bequeathed her art collection—comprising more than 600 twentieth-century paintings and sculptures—to Yale University's art collection. This led to discussions of expanding the existing 1928 gallery to accommodate the Dreier Collection, and thus the architect Philip Goodwin was hired to design a modern addition. A few years earlier, Goodwin, in collaboration with Edward Durell Stone, had designed the new building for the Museum of Modern Art in New York. The Yale project was interrupted during World War II and resumed again in 1950. By this time,

however, the building committee felt the addition was too expensive, and Goodwin was having health problems, deciding therefore to withdraw from the commission. What worked to Kahn's advantage was the fact that the committee and the university had already decided on a modern addition for the historical building.

Kahn was offered the commission in 1951, while he was in residence at the American Academy in Rome. His role was that of designer, while Douglas Orr—a local architect who was already involved with Yale—worked on the early stages of the architectural program and the construction drawings. In many ways, Kahn was an ideal candidate for the project, for he had been teaching at Yale since 1947 and had been awarded the prestigious Rome Prize. When Kahn returned to the United States later in 1951, he collaborated on the design of the Art Gallery addition with Anne Griswold

Tyng, an associate from his office who played a major role in the project. Kahn's interest in Buckminster Fuller geometries (tetrahedral and octahedral forms) was awakened on account of Tyng's own work for a small school and a house for her parents that employed both of these modulated systems.

1954–1959 · Jewish Community Center
Trenton, New Jersey

Central Courtyard of Bathhouse, ca. 1957

The Jewish Community Center in Trenton, New Jersey, illustrates Kahn's interest in repetitive geometries that, in plan, are configured in bilaterally symmetrical compositions. While only a small portion of this vast complex was realized, the building demonstrates that—even with the smallest budgets—pure shapes can be beautifully configured to heighten architecture's sense of spirituality. This is best illustrated by the Bathhouse Pavilion, which is composed of four square forms with pyramidal roofs that are arranged around a central, open courtyard. The proportions of these pavilions and their relationship to the void of the courtyard create a spatial condition in plan that is taken up again most notably in the public atrium space of Kahn's 1972 Library at Phillips Exeter Academy in Exeter, New Hampshire.

Exterior view of covered pavilion

During the course of the Jewish Community Center project in Trenton, New Jersey, Kahn produced four design proposals. He was eager to have the main community structure of the complex realized, as it would have been his first major freestanding building. H. Harvey Saaz, chairman of the construction committee, hired Kahn. Saaz was a Yale alumnus and knew of Kahn's recent success with the Yale University Art Gallery addition. Over time, however, Saaz became the sole supporter of Kahn's vision. Unfortunately, by 1957, Saaz had fallen ill and was forced to abandon his role on the construction committee, leaving the group with no direction or support for Kahn's vast complex project. The commission's final decision was to have a smaller structure erected—the Bathhouse Pavilion.

Entrance view of Bathhouse interior

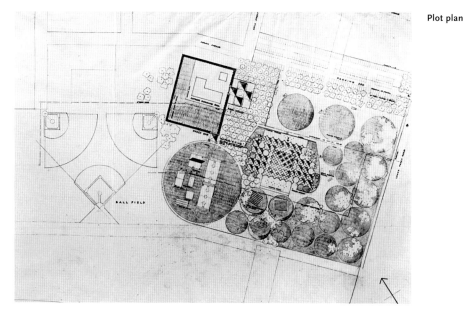

Plot plan

Exterior view of building

Right:
Interior view of Jewish Community Center,
early rendering

1957–1961 ► Alfred Newton Richards Medical Research Building

University of Pennsylvania ► Philadelphia, Pennsylvania

Early sketch of exterior massing

In Kahn's design for the Alfred Newton Richards Medical Research Building, he employed a series of square pavilion forms in the plan—as seen earlier in the design for the Jewish Community Center in Trenton, New Jersey. However, here the square pavilions are multistory buildings with cantilevered corners, and are centrally flanked by monumental brick towers, which house mechanical systems and stairways. The exterior of the cantilevered corners of these square floor plates—which contain the research and lab facilities—is articulated with modulated windowpanes and brick infill. These concrete cantilevered structures are supported by concrete columns that appear rather inconspicuous next to the dominating monolithic brick towers. The objective of this design was to liberate the interior of the building from physical interruptions, enabling the labs to be reconfigured as technology changed. This was achieved by the employment of a deep floor-to-ceiling plate that relegated all research and mechanical systems to be fed through these spaces, without interrupting the lab configuration.

Right page:
Exterior view

Left:
Detailed view of segmented exterior massing

Below left:
Plan

Below right:
Detailed view of cantilevered corners

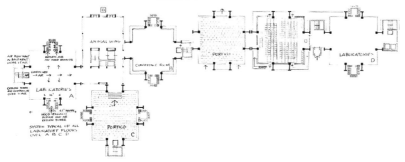

1959–1961 ▸ Esherick House
Philadelphia, Pennsylvania

Left page:
Rear façade

Right:
Front façade

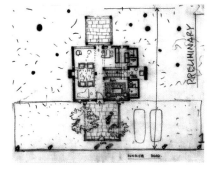

Plan/sketch

Kahn's Esherick House is one of his first realized residential designs to illustrate his formal ideology following his return to the United States from Rome after having been made a Fellow of the American Academy there in 1953. Designed for a single woman, the house has a simple design with a central stair hall, as well as a two-story living room and a fireplace. The overall shape of this two-story dwelling is rectangular. The window articulation and the symmetrical entrance, however, reveal design concepts employed earlier by Kahn, in his public, institutional, and civic architecture, where major and minor façade fenestrations make a monumental impression in their overall composition. Window surfaces are both flush with the façades and deeply recessed into the building's volume. In plan, the Esherick House appears to have thick walls that become carved out to accommodate either bookshelves or recessed windows that are flush with the interior walls. The house's concrete-block construction is stuccoed over to give it the appearance of a monolithic surface, and appears rather elegant in combination with the wood frames of the surface fenestration.

1959–1965·Salk Institute for Biological Studies

La Jolla, California

Left page:
Detailed view of exterior courtyard stairs

The Salk Institute for Biological Studies is possibly Kahn's most poetic and important building designed in the United States. Situated in La Jolla, California, on a bluff overlooking the Pacific Ocean, the structure boasts an outdoor courtyard that evokes the majesty of a cathedral and features simple elements, such as a narrow channel of water that runs down its central plaza and cascades down into a series of pools below. The proportions of this exterior courtyard—its width compared with the vertical height of the adjacent Study Towers—create a beautiful scale that is timeless in character. The symmetrically positioned Study Towers, which rise up on either side of the courtyard, feature 45° angle walls that afford spectacular views. These vertical four-story pavilion-like elements are linked to the larger lab buildings that demarcate the boundary of this vast complex. The highly controlled form-work of the poured-in-place concrete gives rise to an elegant modulation of surfaces that at times are juxtaposed with panels of teak wood, lending scale to the courtyard as well as a sense of monumental grandeur to the overall complex.

In 1959, Jonas Salk—founder of the Salk Institute—was looking for a suitable architect to design his new Institute for Biological Studies in San Diego, California. A friend of Salk's heard Kahn give a lecture and suggested that Salk might like his ideas on architecture. When Kahn and Salk met, they realized they had similar intellectual interests, and Kahn was hired. No formal program was stipulated by Salk; rather, it grew out of his conversation with Kahn about how Salk envisaged the facility. The land for the Salk Institute was provided by the City of San Diego. Salk was offered a variety

View of exterior massing of building

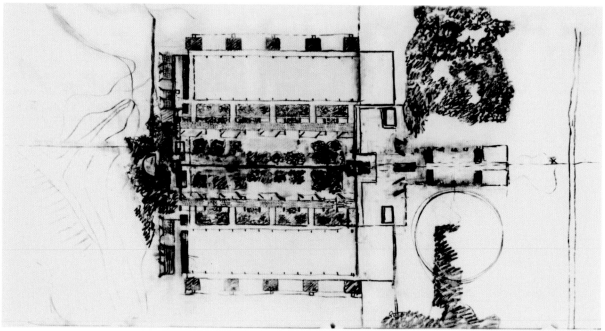

Office/study

Left page above:
Exterior view

Left page below:
Earlier sketch with vegetation in central courtyard

of locations to select from and took Kahn with him to choose the parcel. The chosen site was a stunning coastal cliff parcel in the La Jolla area. Kahn proceeded to produce numerous proposals for its master plan before settling on the realized version. However, by 1965, the cost of construction had exceeded $14 million, the master plan had not been completed, and fellows housing as well as other ancillary structures had not been realized. The commitment that both Kahn and Salk made early in the project provided a concise template from which to complete the master plan for the institute as it grew in scale and majesty.

Entrance and central courtyard

Right:
Detail of oversized water gutter at exterior lower level reflecting pool

Left page:
View across pool to a Study Tower

1959–1969 · First Unitarian Church and School

Rochester, New York

Overall exterior view of building

Most of Kahn's designs have a spiritual character, devoid of program and function. This is emblematic of how he articulates a building's formal massing and its relationship to light. Kahn's First Unitarian Church and School, in Rochester, New York, combines a symbolic design with a program that is a model for modern religious architecture. The building's simple, rhythmic exterior is reminiscent of the ruins of ancient Roman architecture. Symmetrical in plan, with an asymmetrical entrance, the building's principal public space is the congregation area, which is flanked by a series of ancillary rooms screened off by concrete-block parapet walls. To heighten the visual effect, the congregation area is also surrounded by a series of light shafts. The concrete ceiling of this space is bilaterally symmetrical and slopes inward, converging at the center of the room and recalling inverted vaulting. Clad in brick, with few horizontal elements articulated, the building appears much larger—and therefore more monumental—in scale than it actually is.

Interior view

Plan

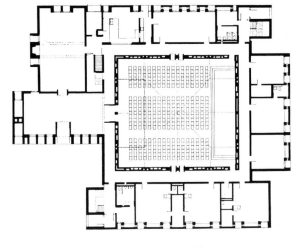

1960–1965 ▸ Eleanor Donnelley Erdman Hall

Bryn Mawr College ▸ Bryn Mawr, Pennsylvania

The overall composition of the building illustrates Kahn's ability to contextualize on a historical campus as well as produce a new formal dormitory typology. The three highly geometric forms that comprise the complex are situated along an axis of public interior spaces that are flanked by private rooms. This sequential arrangement of public interior spaces is also explored in Kahn's later, larger buildings in Bangladesh and India. In many ways, this was an ideal program for Kahn to explore the formal relationship between grand public spaces enclosed by less significant spaces, such as sleeping quarters.

Public gathering spaces—dining halls as well as numerous reception rooms—were central to the program of this all-female university and one of the main requirements determined by Katharine Elizabeth McBride, president of the institution for almost twenty years when she hired Kahn. Prior to awarding the commission to Kahn, she had also considered Richard Neutra and Marcel Breuer for the project. Even though Kahn's progressive design ideology was welcome, to a certain extent he nevertheless had to work within the neo-Gothic aesthetic of the campus (established earlier by architects Walter Cope and John Stewardson), stipulating that gray stone wall surfaces and white limestone (characteristic of the earlier buildings) had to be used. Also, in keeping with the aesthetic guidelines of the earlier dormitory rooms on the campus, these spaces required window seats; and in order to prevent students from defacing the walls with nails when hanging up family pictures, they had to conceal hanging molding, which was installed where the wall met the ceiling.

Aerial view

Looking up at balcony in Central Hall

Left:
Interior view looking out from balcony into Central Hall

View of main entrance

Below:
Plan

From the outside, the building is a modern gem within the context of a historical setting. The highly geometric composition of the plan is only slightly revealed in its modulated façades. The vertically articulated white limestone corners of the buildings contrast with narrower horizontal datums of the same material, reducing the wall massing, while drawing attention to the datum zone of the dormitory windows.

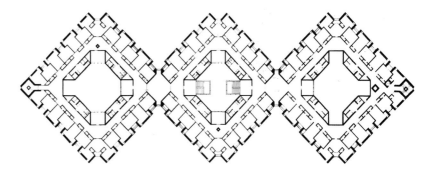

1960–1967 · Fisher House
Hatboro, Pennsylvania

Left page:
Rear façade

Right:
Entrance hall and living room

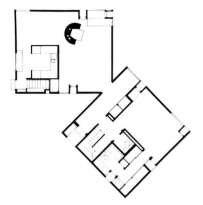

Plan

To accommodate its gently sloping site, Kahn fitted the Fisher House with a stone base to make up for the change in grade and provides a lower level that opens onto the property. The exterior is quite extraordinary—two cubic volumes, one that is situated at a 45° angle to the other, with a tenuous connection between them, which results in a dynamic configuration. The house is clad mainly in vertical wood siding. Reminiscent of the Yale University Art Gallery addition, a narrow horizontal datum of wood is employed on the façades to demarcate the second floor of the volume. The most complex aspect of these façades is the arrangement of the windows, which feature large spans of glass juxtaposed with deep recesses containing smaller windows. This results in an abstract geometry, which also reveals itself inside the house, with elements such as an intricately composed window seat in the living room. The only angled surface in the orthogonally placed cubic volume is the stone fireplace in the living room, which reiterates the 45° angle of the adjacent cubic volume.

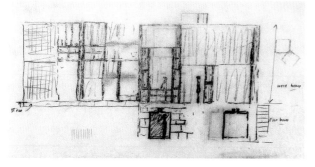

Side façade

Left:
Early sketch

Right page:
Living room with fireplace

1962–1974 ▸ Indian Institute of Management
Ahmedabad, Gujarat, India

Left page:

Auditorium wing (left in picture) and the adjoining library (right)

Kahn and Dr. Samuel Paul on site
Dr. Paul became Director of the Indian Institute of Management after 1972.

One of Kahn's few realized commissions outside the United States—which showcases his ability as an urban planner and architect on a vast scale—was the Indian Institute of Management in Ahmedabad, India. Begun in 1962 (the same year Kahn received an even larger commission for Sher-e-Bangla Nagar, the Capital of Bangladesh), this project took over a decade to complete. Kahn, however, was able to see most of the final buildings completed in his last trip to India in March of 1974, prior to his death upon returning to the United States from this visit.

The program for this project called for numerous building types—a school, dormitories, and faculty and servant housing—all to be situated on a sixty-five-acre site that was relatively flat, empty farmland miles away from any existing urban developments. Kahn took this barren landscape and created a site plan that is a study in scale proportions inherent in geometric forms and related them to the institutional hierarchy of these different buildings and their programs. Contrary to the mainstream minimal modern aesthetic, where a building's programs—dormitory versus school—are identified solely by their signage, Kahn's buildings became meta-narratives of their programs, allowing these typologies to be juxtaposed. This is evident, for example, in the scale and monumental massing of the school building, which contrasts with the repetitive exterior of the dormitory buildings, which are lower in height. The one unifying element of these two formal typologies was the employment of diagonal wall surfaces. This has been employed subtly at the four corners of the school building, while it is the

major organizing principle in the interior of the dormitory buildings. This highly con-trolled geometric massing of the school and dormitory buildings—which are separ-ated from all other buildings by an asymmetrical man-made lake—is carried over to the staff and servant housing buildings, which are much lower in height.

Passage between student dormitories

The scale of this vast campus setting for the Indian Institute of Management was determined by the government of India and the western state of Gujarat, and modeled after Harvard Business School. The commission was originally offered to Balkrishna Vithaldas Doshi, a local practicing architect of prominence who taught at the National Institute of Design. He had originally moved to Ahmedabad to oversee the construc-tion of Le Corbusier's Museum for the Cultural Center of Ahmedabad, which was com-pleted in 1956. Doshi had met Kahn earlier in Philadelphia and knew the significance of his work and what this commission would be both for Kahn and for India, and sugges-ted that he be awarded the commission. Doshi's own office acted as the local architect collaborating on this vast program of buildings. However, the magnitude of the pro-ject—the bureaucratic cultural differences, the climate, the time difference, the dead-lines, etc.—led to a situation that was less than ideal, with construction beginning before Kahn had actually completed the designs. In 1969, the client requested Kahn to make a special visit back to India (which he did infrequently), otherwise the execution of the remaining complex would be turned over to the local architect of the project,

Dormitories

Right:
Site plan, January 2, 1975, drawn at the office of the architect Anant D. Raje (who worked continously with Kahn as an associate from the beginning of the project)

1. Library
2. Faculty office
3. Classroom
4. Service tower
5. Dormitories
6. Lake
7. Kitchen and dining room
8. Faculty residence
9. Married students' residence
10. Management development center

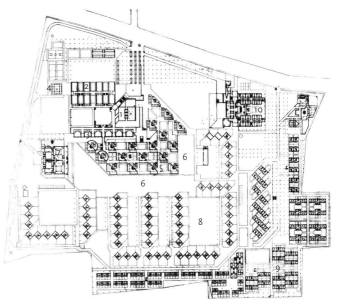

Hallway in educational facility

Doshi. Kahn made the visit and the site architect, Anant D. Raje, who worked with both Kahn's and Doshi's offices to coordinate their efforts, took on a larger role in the remaining time.

To both Doshi's and Raje's credit, Raje likewise visited Kahn's office in Philadelphia to pick up working drawings for buildings with similar detailing and to take them back to ensure Kahn's original quality. Owing to the time it took to finalize and execute these buildings, many other buildings by Kahn had already been realized. Hence, the Indian Institute of Management campus can be seen as an assembly of buildings from Kahn's oeuvre. However, the quality of the local construction and brick was poor compared to that of his buildings erected in the United States.

Administrative passageway

Hallway through dormitories on
 elevated level

Left page above:
Dormitories

Left page below:
Longitudinal site section

Courtyard with administrative wing on left,
library center, and auditorium on right

1962–1983·Government sector

Sher-e-Bangla Nagar, Dhaka, Bangladesh

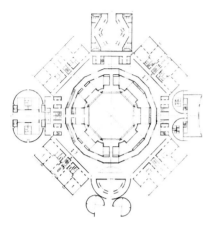

National Assembly Building, plan

Kahn is one of the few architects of the twentieth century to have a body of built work comprising important designs—featuring a variety of building typologies—that has allowed the discipline to reflect upon and reevaluate earlier models of modern architecture. His design for the capital of Bangladesh is his most important contribution. In many ways, one can see his earlier projects as building up to this significant achievement in Kahn's architecture, which is highly formal, monumental, and spiritual in character. Over the twenty years that it took to realize his vision, Kahn's project experienced a number of interruptions and delays—the longest of which was due to the Bangladesh Liberation War of 1971–1972. The most important part of this project, the National Assembly Building, was finally completed in 1982—eight years after the architect's death.

The commission was on a truly grand scale. Situated on 1,000 acres in a flat landscape—adjacent to the airport—the site was known to flood periodically during the monsoon season. Prior to Kahn, the project was offered to Le Corbusier, who had already designed numerous buildings in the region, and Alvar Aalto—however, both had declined. Kahn readily accepted the commission in 1962. A site office was set up, but most of the designing took place in his Philadelphia office. Kahn had Roy Vollmer (from his Philadelphia office) move to Dhaka to run the site office as the project got underway. This may reflect his unsuccessful collaboration with a local architect on the Indian Institute of Management in Ahmedabad, India.

Kahn first visited the site in 1963, when the local building authorities had given permission to start work on 200 acres of the site. The buildings for this part of the master plan included residences for assembly members, secretaries, government ministers, and staff, as well as private residences for the president and speakers. The largest and most important building for this parcel of land, however, was the National Assembly Building. The program for the National Assembly Building alone was enormous, with a 300-seat assembly chamber, a prayer hall, a dining hall, and a mosque, as well as a large outdoor area for large ceremonial events. The remaining 800 acres were earmarked for a hospital, schools, a market, a museum, etc.—all the building typologies that comprise the fabric of a capital city—to be conceived and planned by Kahn in a later, second phase.

The overall master plan for the first phase of 200 acres is a geometric study in symmetrical compositions with smaller asymmetrical configurations. Kahn took two years to develop it. This enabled him to become better acquainted with the harsh climate, the regional architecture, and local construction techniques as well as the site conditions. Kahn's sensitive reading of the site and the cultural importance of the National Assembly Building within it are reflected in the man-made lake adjacent to the structure. While this feature was designed to act as a large basin to regulate excess seasonal water, it also provided a surface on which the building could be mirrored, creating a striking image of horizontal symmetry.

The overall composition of the National Assembly Building is a study in beauty and complexity, and it incorporates elements that protect enclosed and outdoor spaces

Exterior view from northwest at reflecting pool

from the sun. The monumental scale of the extruded forms that collectively comprise the perimeter of the building is further emphasized by oversized circular and triangular shapes that are cut out from the wall surfaces to reveal a spatial complexity beyond these exterior surfaces. Kahn's employment of marble and concrete was used in part to heighten the building's monumental scale and to form a counterpoint to the other buildings, which are lower in height, constructed with brick, and symmetrically arranged along the edge of the man-made lake.

Interestingly, Kahn achieved his greatest vision for a city located in one of the poorest countries in the world. For the government of Bangladesh, he established a new

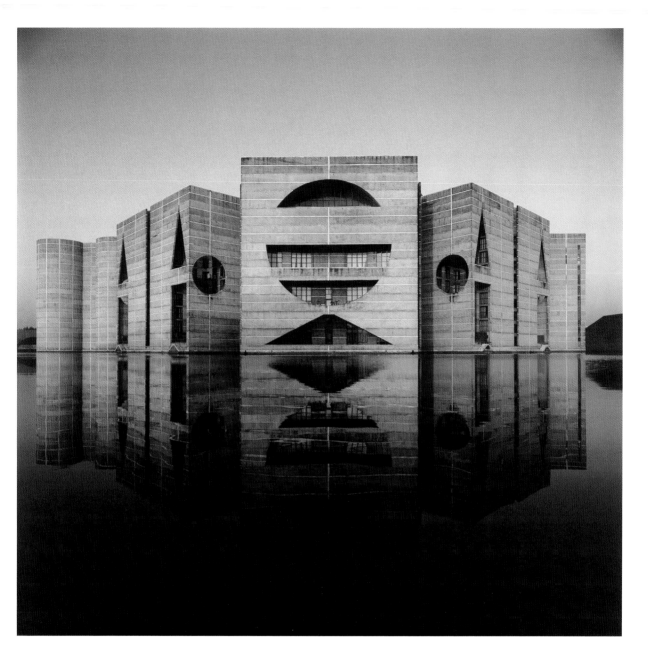

Exterior view from southeast

visual idiom and the construction standards needed to realize the National Assembly Building, as well as other timeless structures planned to be erected in the vast capital long after the architect's death.

View of intricate geometric
ceiling plane

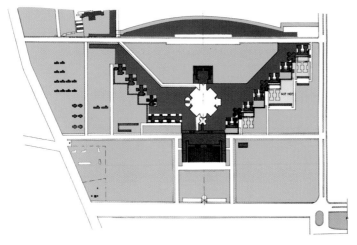

Site plan

Assembly Chamber

View of office blocks are separated
from the National Assembly complex by
a man-made lake

Right:
Hospital, interior view of covered arcade

Right page above:
View of east hostels

Right page below:
Elevation studies of wall openings

1965–1971 ▸ Library
Phillips Exeter Academy ▸ Exeter, New Hampshire

The Phillips Exeter Library is one of Kahn's most visually austere and important buildings for an American educational institution. While the façades are almost elemental in character, the interior volumes, massing, and overall geometries reveal the influence of Kahn's design for the National Assembly Building in Dhaka, Bangladesh (which was commissioned in 1962 and finished after his death in 1974).

Kahn's track record for successful new buildings situated within existing campus settings, such as those at Yale University, the University of Pennsylvania, the Salk Institute, and Bryn Mawr College as well as his unbuilt proposals for Rice University, the Maryland Institute College of Art, and the Philadelphia College of Art, made him one of the most sought-after and prominent architects for this type of commission. As with many of Kahn's earlier campus commissions, the new principal at Phillips Exeter Academy, Richard W. Day, wanted a modern building that would offset the historical character of the other campus buildings, thus making a significant contribution to the campus's architectural landscape. A shortlist of possible candidates was compiled, which included Kahn, Edward Larrabee Barnes, Paul Rudolph, and Philip Johnson. After the committee visited the offices of these architects and inspected some of their built work, Kahn was offered the commission. The projected cost of building Kahn's design exceeded the initial budget of $2.5 million, which required that the design be altered rather radically—the entire top floor had to be omitted. After numerous meetings with and letters to the committee in which the architect persuasively warned that such a change would significantly alter the overall scale of the design, the committee agreed to raise additional funds; and in the final round of modifications to the working drawings, the top floor was reinstated.

Exterior view

Below:
Study carrel

Perspective sketch of roof gardens, 1967
Seminar room (left), head-high balustrade with
benches (right)

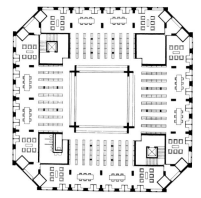

Plan of second floor

The resulting design is one of exact and elegant proportions that is timeless in character and one of the Academy's most beautiful campus buildings. The exterior brick screen-like walls—which visually demarcate this seemingly simple building mass—comprise brick piers that rise from floor to floor. On the second, third, and fourth floors are private reading carrels (which are arranged around the perimeter of the building) that are located within these spaces between the brick piers and are articulated on the façade as an intermediate horizontal datum of wood paneling with a small window in each carrel.

The Exeter Library boasts one of the most extraordinary interior spaces created by Kahn in the United States—a large volumetric void. While this empty space might appear cavernous in the plan and sectional drawings, in reality the spatial complexity of this interior space, ranging from the circular cutouts of the four wall surfaces to the ceiling, which terminates with large diagonal concrete cross-beams, is reminiscent of earlier library designs celebrating vast central spaces, such as Etienne-Louis Boullée's 1785 project for a Royal Library, or Erik Gunnar Asplund's 1927 Public Library in Stockholm.

1966–1972 ▸ Kimbell Art Museum

Fort Worth, Texas

Left page:
Entrance at garden

When the Kimbell Art Museum was officially opened to the public in 1972, it marked another aesthetic achievement in the oeuvre of Louis I. Kahn and introduced a new institution with a considerable presence in Texas, and indeed, the art world at large. Situated in a park setting, the museum's nine-and-a-half-acre trapezoidal site is adjacent to other prominent museums, most notably the Amon Carter Museum, designed by Philip Johnson, which opened in 1961.

Mr. and Mrs. Kay Kimbell, after whom the institution is named, established a foundation to erect an art museum to house their growing collection. The board of the Kimbell Art Foundation—which had been established as early as 1936—hired Richard F. Brown as director of the museum in 1965 to realize the vision of and conceive a program for the institution as well as augment its collection. Brown selected Kahn for the commission; however, the contract required that the architect collaborate with Preston M. Geren & Associates, a local architectural firm.

As with many institutions that realize their first building, the program took into account the future goals of the museum, allocating vast space to the expanding art collection, which would put the institution on the map and make it one of the city's major attractions.

Kahn, who never settled for easy or first solutions, took three years to produce four design proposals for the museum. The one leitmotif running through all his proposals was the employment of horizontal cycloid roofs/ceilings. As with most of his buildings, Kahn managed to come up with features that contextualized and lent a unique character to the project. The signature roofs/ceilings are just such examples, firmly associating the structure with the once rural setting of Fort Worth. Specifically, in the distance—and at one time visible from the site—was a grain silo (which has since been torn down). Ideologically, one can see and better understand how the overall form of a grain silo (which is comprised of a series of vaulted forms separated by a flat surface) conceptually deplaced from its vertical condition and resituated horizontally in the landscape, becomes the framework for the roof/ceiling configuration. These cycloid forms—be they employed vertically or horizontally—are the very elements that characterize and contextualize the Kimbell Art Museum in its Texas landscape.

Another feature that recurs throughout the design is diffuse light let in through skylights that run the length of each vaulted ceiling. This is one of the most striking aspects of the building's end-wall elevations, which profile these repetitive roof forms. To convey the inherent differences and qualities in materials, the arch of the concrete roof/ceiling is radially offset from the curve of the adjacent travertine-clad wall. The resulting space between these curvatures forms a transom, which allows oblique rays of light into the rooms. These rhythmic roof forms, which can be seen on two of the building's four façades, provide a lively visual impression when walking up the stepped ramp leading to the museum's main entrance.

Overall exterior view of building's repetitive massing

Left:
Site plan sketch showing the relation of open and covered spaces, 1967

View of garden entrance with cascading
fountains in the foreground

Right:
Plan

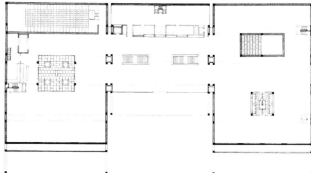

Interior view of gallery

Left:
View from the stage in the auditorium

Interior view of gallery

Right:
Louis Kahn on site

1969–1974 · Yale Center for British Art
New Haven, Connecticut

Detailed view of ceiling at Library Court

Situated across the street from his 1951–1953 Yale University Art Gallery addition, Kahn's Yale Center for British Art has a simple, restrained exterior aesthetic that makes the building blend in with the urban fabric of New Haven. The Center's interior spaces are visually warm, and incorporate features recalling those of galleries from the seventeenth and eighteenth centuries, albeit rendered with a contemporary palette of poured-in-place concrete, stainless steel, and wood panels.

In 1966, the philanthropist and art collector Paul Mellon announced that funds would be set aside to erect a new facility at Yale University to house his collection of British art—which includes work ranging from the early seventeenth to the mid-nineteenth century—and that an endowment would be created to support fellowships for students researching these periods. In 1968, Yale president Kingman Brewster recommended that the Mellon gift be folded into a larger center comprising an art gallery, libraries, and research facilities. The site for the building was suggested by the architect Edward Larrabee Barnes, who served as a consultant to Brewster. Barnes was also influential in the selection of Kahn for the project, having suggested him to Jules

Interior view of galleries

D. Prown—director of the Paul Mellon Centre for Studies in British Art at Yale. Prown had been appointed by Brewster to commission an architect and oversee the project. Kahn was officially hired by the university in 1969.

By 1971, Kahn had developed three distinct proposals. One important element of the commission—which appeared in all proposals—was the inclusion of retail space at street level. New storefronts were to replace those that had been demolished to make way for the new building. Retaining the street character provided by retail spaces was essential to win the support of the local and student community.

The final built version of the Yale Center for British Art has a very discreet corner entrance that is recessed at the base of the building behind the retail footprint of the building. When entering the center, a four-story space reveals the institution. The coffered ceiling allows indirect light to fill the space. Adjacent to the entrance court on the second floor is another, larger interior court designed to exhibit artworks. The only architectural element occupying this majestic space is a cylindrical stairwell that makes reference to Kahn's Art Gallery addition across the street. Structural framing members for the building's skylight were nearly in place when Kahn died, in 1974. Thereafter, the

Interior view of conservation lab

university hired architects Anthony Pellechia and Marshall D. Meyers to complete the center, both of whom had worked for Kahn and supervised earlier commissions. The Yale Center for British Art was officially completed in 1977.

1971–1973 ▸ Korman House
Fort Washington, Pennsylvania

Left page:
Exterior view of house in the landscape

Right:
Front façade

Living room

The Korman House was the last residence designed by Kahn. The project, with which he was commissioned in 1971, was actually for two homes on adjacent lots. However, the Honickman House—the other residence—was not realized. This is unfortunate because its plan indicates several spaces with trapezoidal walls that, in Kahn's hands, could have become interesting domestic spaces indeed.

The Korman House was a much more normative design. The program for this house was vast, with five bedrooms and rooms for guests. In its overall layout, Kahn kept to his ideology of discrete "public" and "private" zones within the home (this idea can be seen already in his design for the Oser House, 1939–1943). In the "public" zone of the home, the living room and dining room are articulated as a two-story volume with symmetrically arranged fireplaces at either end. The more "private" bedrooms and bathrooms comprise the remaining massing of the home and are arranged around the formal two-story entrance hall. The exterior is clad with simple materials, such as vertical siding and fieldstone, which by this point in Kahn's career had become his signature palette of brilliantly detailed materials. The design of the Korman House went through numerous versions, and the realized proposal is rather demure compared to the initial design.

Life and Work

Louis and Esther Kahn in August 1930

1901 ▸ Born February 20 in Estonia

1904 ▸ Father, Leopold, moves to the United States and settles in Philadelphia

1906 ▸ Mother, Bertha, moves to Philadelphia with son Louis and his siblings

1915 ▸ Louis I. Kahn becomes a naturalized American citizen

1920–1924 ▸ Student at the University of Pennsylvania, School of Fine Arts, receiving a Bachelor of Architecture degree

1921–1922 ▸ Works for Hoffman-Henon Co., Philadelphia, PA

1922 ▸ Works for Hewitt & Ash Architects, Philadelphia, PA

1925–1926 ▸ Works for John Molitor, City Architect, Philadelphia, PA

1927–1928 ▸ Works for William H. Lee Architect, Philadelphia, PA

1928–1929 ▸ Travels around Europe (Austria, Czechoslovakia, Denmark, England, Estonia, Finland, France, Germany, Hungary, Italy, Latvia, Lithuania, Sweden, Switzerland, and The Netherlands)

1929–1930 ▸ Works for Paul P. Cret, Architect, Philadelphia, PA

1930 ▸ Marries Esther Virginia Israeli; one child, Sue Ann, in 1940

1930–1932 ▸ Works for Zantzinger, Borie & Medary Architects, Philadelphia, PA

1934 ▸ Establishes his own office in Philadelphia, PA
Buten Paint Store, Philadelphia, PA

1937
Ahavath Israel Synagogue, Philadelphia, PA
Waldman Dental Office, Philadelphia, PA

1940
Abraham Apartment and Dental Office, Philadelphia, PA
Battery Workers Union, Local 113, Philadelphia, PA

1941 ▸ Forms a partnership with George Howe (Howe and Kahn). Later that year, the office is expanded to include Oscar Stonorov (Howe, Stonorov, and Kahn)

1942 ▸ Howe leaves the partnership, which continues to operate until 1947 under the name Stonorov and Kahn

1943
International Ladies Garment Workers Union Health Center, Philadelphia, PA
Lily Ponds Houses, Washington, DC
Oser House, Elkins Park, PA
Pine Ford Acres Housing Development, Middletown, PA
Pennypack Woods Housing, Philadelphia, PA

1944 ▸ Kahn publishes "Monumentality" in *New Architecture and City Planning*, edited by Paul Zucker, New York, Philosophical Library
Carver Court Housing Development, Coatesville, PA
Lincoln Highway Defense Housing Development, Coatesville, PA
National Jewish Welfare Board, Washington, DC

1945
Bernard House, Philadelphia, PA
Industrial Union of Marine and Shipbuilding Workers of America, Local 1, Camden, NJ
Moskalik House, Philadelphia, PA

1946
Department of Neurology, Jefferson Medical College, Philadelphia, PA
Gimbels Department Store, Philadelphia, PA
Radbill House, Merion, PA

1947
William H. Harman Corporation Prefabricated Houses, West Chester, PA

Louis Kahn lecturing at the University of Pennsylvania, 1971
Kahn possessed the ability to draw with both hands at the same time.

International Ladies Garment Workers Union, Pike County, PA
Memorial Playground, Western Home for Children, Philadelphia, PA
Radbill Oil Company, Philadelphia, PA

1947–1957 ▶ Professor of Architecture at Yale University, New Haven, CT

1948
X-Ray Department, Graduate Hospital, University of Pennsylvania, Philadelphia, PA

1949
Coward Shoe Store, Philadelphia, PA
Roche House, Conshohocken, PA

1950
Weiss House, East Norriton Township, PA

1950–1951 ▶ Resident at the American Academy in Rome

1951
American Federation of Labor Health Center, St. Luke's Hospital, Philadelphia, PA
Pincus Occupational Therapy Building, Philadelphia Psychiatric Hospital, Philadelphia, PA
Genel House, Wynnewood, PA
Leidner House, Elkins Park, PA

1953 ▶ Made a Fellow of the American Institute of Architects (FAIA)
Yale University Art Gallery, New Haven, CT

1954 ▶ Fathers a child, Alexandra Tyng, with Anne Griswold Tyng
Samuel Radbill Building, Philadelphia Psychiatric Hospital, Philadelphia, PA
Jewish Community Center, New Haven, CT

1955 ▶ Kahn publishes "Order is" in *Perspecta,* no. 3
Adler House, Philadelphia, PA

1956
Mill Creek Housing / Phase 1, Philadelphia, PA
Wharton Esherick Workshop, Paoli, PA

1957
American Federation of Labor Medical Services Building, Philadelphia, PA

1957–1974 ▶ Professor of Architecture, University of Pennsylvania, Philadelphia, PA

1958
Zoob and Matz Offices, Philadelphia, PA

1959
Jewish Community Center, Trenton, NJ
Shaw House, Philadelphia, PA

1961
Barge for the American Wind Symphony Orchestra, River Thames, England
Esherick House, Philadelphia, PA

1962
Clever House, Cherry Hill, NJ
Shapiro House, Narberth, PA
Tribune Review Publishing Company Building, Greensburg, PA
Center of Philadelphia, Philadelphia, PA

1963 ▶ Fathers a child, Nathaniel Kahn, with Harriet Pattison
Mill Creek Housing / Phase 2, Philadelphia, PA

1965
Alfred Newton Richards Medical Research Building and Biology Building, University of Pennsylvania, Philadelphia, PA
Eleanor Donnelley Erdman Hall, Bryn Mawr College, Bryn Mawr, PA
Salk Institute for Biological Studies, La Jolla, CA

1966 ▶ Retrospective exhibition at the Museum of Modern Art, New York

1967
Barge for the American Wind Symphony Orchestra, Pittsburgh, PA
Fisher House, Hatboro, PA

Kahn at the National Institute of Design in Ahmedabad, India, 1967
The men in the photo are not students, rather colleagues who assisted Kahn with the design of the Indian Institute of Management.

1969
First Unitarian Church and School, Rochester, NY

1970
Olivetti-Underwood Factory, Harrisburg, PA

1971
President's House, University of Pennsylvania, Philadelphia, PA

1972
Kimbell Art Museum, Fort Worth, TX
Library, Phillips Exeter Academy, Exeter, NH
Temple Beth-El Synagogue, Chappaqua, NY

1973
Fine Arts Center, School, and Performing Arts Theater, Fort Wayne, IN
Korman House, Fort Washington, PA

1974 ▸ March 17, dies of a heart attack in New York City
Indian Institute of Management, Ahmedabad, India
Wolfson Center for Mechanical and Transportation Engineering Buildings, Tel Aviv, Israel
Yale Center for British Art, New Haven, CT

1975
Family Planning Center and Maternal Health Center, Kathmandu, Nepal

1983
Government sector with National Assembly Building, Sher-e-Bangla Nagar, Dhaka, Bangladesh

USA

Bryn Mawr, Pennsylvania
Eleanor Donnelley Erdman Hall

Coatesville, Pennsylvania
Carver Court Housing

Elkins Park, Pennsylvania
Oser House

Exeter, New Hampshire
Library, Phillips Exeter Academy

Fort Washington, Pennsylvania
Korman House

Fort Worth, Texas
Kimbell Art Museum

Hatboro, Pennsylvania
Fisher House

La Jolla, California
Salk Institute for Biological Studies

New Haven, Connecticut
Yale University Art Gallery
Yale Center for British Art

Philadelphia, Pennsylvania
Center of Philadelphia
Alfred Newton Richards Medical Research
Building
Esherick House

Rochester, New York
First Unitarian Church and School

Trenton, New Jersey
Jewish Community Center

San Francisco

Los Angeles

La Jolla

PACIFIC OCEAN